D1203396

How Toys Roll

Helen Whittaker

Smart Apple Media
P.O. Box 3263
Mankato, MN, 56002

First published in 2011 by
MACMILLAN EDUCATION AUSTRALIA PTY LTD
15–19 Claremont Street, South Yarra 3141

Visit our website at www.macmillan.com.au or go directly to www.macmillanlibrary.com.au

Associated companies and representatives throughout the world.

Library of Congress Cataloging-in-Publication Data has been applied for.

Publisher: Carmel Heron
Commissioning Editor: Niki Horin
Managing Editor: Vanessa Lanaway
Editors: Emma de Smit and Tim Clarke
Proofreader: Helena Newton
Designer: Kerri Wilson
Page layout: Romy Pearse
Photo researcher: Wendy Duncan (management: Debbie Gallagher)
Illustrator: Ned Culic
Production Controller: Vanessa Johnson

Manufactured in China by Macmillan Production (Asia) Ltd.
Kwun Tong, Kowloon, Hong Kong
Supplier Code: CP March 2011

Acknowledgements
The publisher would like to thank Heidi Ruhnau, Head of Science at Oxley College, Victoria, for her assistance in reviewing manuscripts.

The author and publisher are grateful to the following for permission to reproduce copyright material:

Front cover photograph: Boy on skateboard © Getty Images/Joe McBride.

Photographs courtesy of: Corbis/Eyetrigger Pty Ltd, 4 (bottom left), /Henrik Weis, 5 (bottom), /Norbert Schaefer, 5 (top); Getty Images/Mieke Dalle, 8 (right),12, /Flickr/Lucidio Studio, Inc., 9 (bottom left), 16, /iStock Exclusive/David Safanda, 1, /Taxi/Adamsmith, 8 (left), 10; Masterfile/Alice Berber, 6, /Kevin Dodge, 9 (top), 14; MEA Images/Image Source, 4 (bottom centre); photolibrary/Alamy/Aurora Photos, 4 (bottom right), /Edith Held, 9 (right), 18, /Jim Cummins, 20; Pixmac/Yuri Arcurs, 4 (top left); Shutterstock/cassiede alain, 4 (top right), /Michael William, 4 (top centre).

While every care has been taken to trace and acknowledge copyright, the publisher tenders their apologies for any accidental infringement where copyright has proved untraceable. They would be pleased to come to a suitable arrangement with the rightful owner in each case.

Contents

When a word is printed in **bold**, you can look up its meaning in the Glossary on page 31.

Toys and Forces

Forces make toys work. Forces make toys start moving, change direction, speed up, slow down, and stop. Forces also change the shape of some toys.

| Bouncing toys | Floating toys | Flying toys |
| Rolling toys | Sliding toys | Spinning toys |

None of these toys would work without forces.

What Is a Force?

A force is a push or a pull. When you push something, it moves away from you. When you pull something, it moves towards you.

When this girl applies a pushing force to the cart, it moves away from her.

When this boy applies a pulling force to the cart, it moves towards him.

How Does a Rolling Toy Work?

A rolling toy works when a pushing or pulling force makes it move. When the force pushes or pulls the toy, the toy's **wheels** turn. When the wheels turn, the toy rolls.

A pushing force makes these toys move, causing their wheels to turn.

A rolling toy can roll because it has special moving parts. Wheels and **axles** are the moving parts that allow a rolling toy to roll.

Wheels and axles make rolling toys roll easily across the ground.

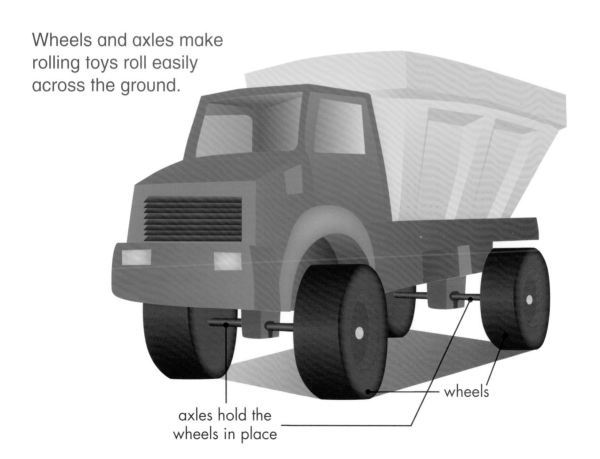

wheels

axles hold the wheels in place

How Do Forces Make Rolling Toys Work?

Different forces make rolling toys work. Pushes and pulls make the toys work in different ways. Forces can make rolling toys work in these ways.

Forces can make rolling toys start moving.

Forces can make rolling toys change direction.

Forces can make rolling toys speed up.

Forces can make rolling toys slow down.

Forces can make rolling toys stop moving.

What Makes a Rolling Toy Start Moving?

When forces act on a rolling toy, they can make it start moving. One force that can make a rolling toy start moving is a pushing force.

An inline skate starts moving when you apply a pushing force with your leg.

You can make a rolling toy start moving by applying a pushing force to the toy. This force makes the toy start moving by making the wheels turn.

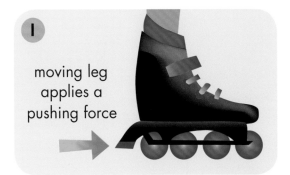

moving leg applies a pushing force

inline skate starts moving

A pushing force acts on an inline skate to make it start moving.

wheels turn

What Makes a Rolling Toy Change Direction?

When forces act on a rolling toy, they can make it change direction. One force that can do this is a **turning force**. A turning force is a push and a pull working together.

A turning force can make a bicycle change direction.

The front wheels on some rolling toys can turn left and right. Applying a turning force to the front wheels will make them turn. This makes the toy change direction.

rider applies turning force to handlebars

turning force

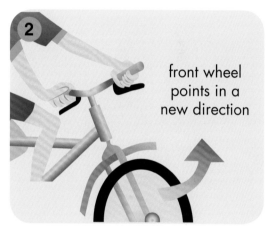

front wheel points in a new direction

A turning force makes the bicycle's handlebars change direction, which makes the front wheel change direction.

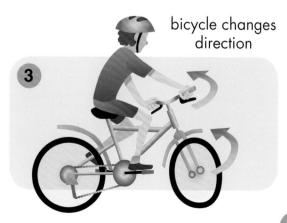

bicycle changes direction

What Makes a Rolling Toy Speed Up?

When forces act on a rolling toy, they can make it speed up. One force that can make a rolling toy speed up is a pulling force.

A pulling force can make a wagon speed up.

You can make a rolling toy speed up by pulling it harder. This applies a larger pulling force to the toy. The larger pulling force makes the wheels turn faster.

1 small pulling force
wagon moves slowly
wheels turn slowly

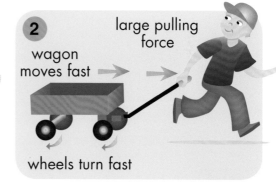

2 large pulling force
wagon moves fast
wheels turn fast

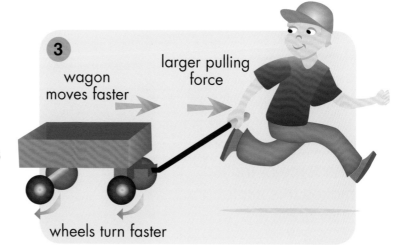

3 larger pulling force
wagon moves faster
wheels turn faster

Pulling harder means a larger force acts on the wagon, so it moves faster.

What Makes a Rolling Toy Slow Down?

When forces act on a rolling toy, they can make it slow down. One force that can slow a rolling toy down is **friction**.

The force of friction makes this skateboard slow down.

Friction occurs between two **surfaces** that are touching one another. With a rolling toy, friction between the wheels and the ground makes the toy slow down.

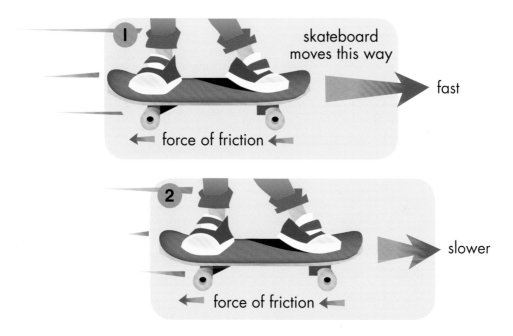

1 | skateboard moves this way | fast
force of friction

2 | slower
force of friction

The force of friction between the wheels and the ground slows the skateboard down.

3 | slow
force of friction

What Makes a Rolling Toy Stop Moving?

When forces act on a rolling toy, they can make it stop moving. One force that can make a rolling toy stop moving is an **impact force**.

If this toy car hits an object it will receive an impact force.

When a rolling toy hits an object, the object applies an impact force. The impact force may be large enough to make the toy stop moving.

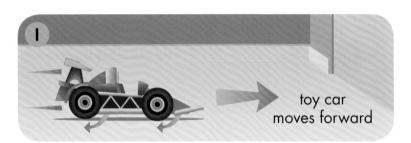

1 toy car moves forward

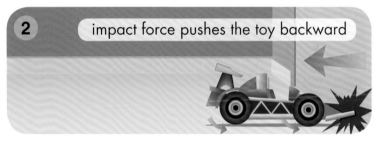

2 impact force pushes the toy backward

impact force

The impact force makes the toy car's wheels stop turning, so the toy car stops.

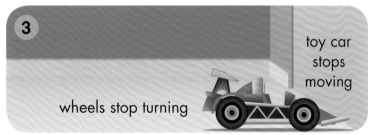

3 toy car stops moving

wheels stop turning

What Else Affects How a Rolling Toy Moves?

A sloped surface can make a rolling toy move faster. A pulling force called **gravity** makes a rolling toy move faster down a slope.

Gravity is the invisible force that pulls the scooter down a slope.

When a rolling toy is on a slope, gravity pulls the toy downward. This makes the toy speed up as it rolls down the slope.

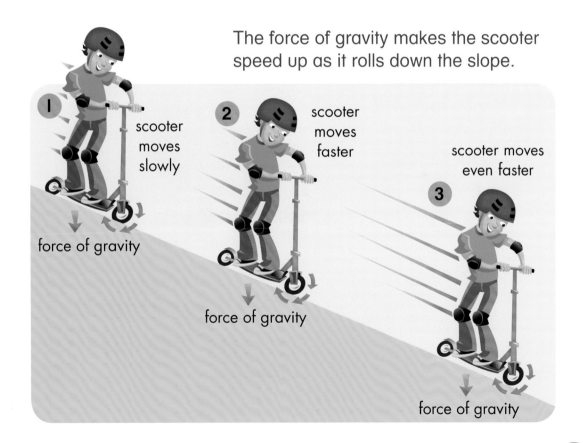

The force of gravity makes the scooter speed up as it rolls down the slope.

1 scooter moves slowly

force of gravity

2 scooter moves faster

force of gravity

scooter moves even faster

3

force of gravity

Make a Rolling Toy: Balloon-powered Racer

This balloon-powered racer is easy to make and fun to play with.

What you need:

- 4 plastic bottle lids
- a drawing compass
- 2 wooden skewers
- scissors
- 6 x 4 inch rectangle of thick cardboard
- 2 straight straws
- sticky tape
- flexible straw
- balloon
- rubber band

Ask a parent or teacher for help.

The force of the air coming out of the balloon pushes the racers along.

What to do:

1 Ask an adult to make a hole in the middle of each bottle lid, using the point of the compass. The hole should be just big enough to fit a skewer through.

2 Cut the points off the skewers using the scissors.

3 Tape the straight straws to the cardboard.

4 Put a skewer through each straw.

5 Put the lids on the ends of the skewers.

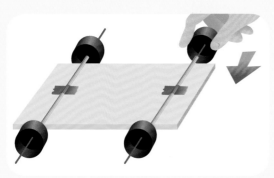

6 Turn the racer the right way up so it is resting on its wheels.

7 Cut the straight end off the flexible straw.

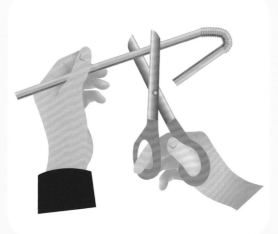

8 Fix the balloon to the flexible straw using the rubber band.

9 Tape the flexible straw to the racer.

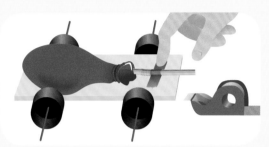

10 Blow through the flexible straw to blow up the balloon. Pinch the flexible straw to keep the air in.

11 Let go of the flexible straw and watch the racer go!

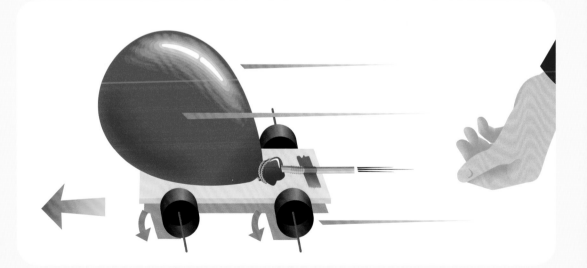

Experiment: How Far Will It Go?

Try this experiment to find out how friction affects the distance a rolling toy can travel.

What you need:

- wooden board
- books
- rolling toy (you could use your balloon-powered racer, but do not blow up the balloon)
- straws for measuring
- paper
- pencil
- ruler

What to do:

1 Choose some different surfaces to test. They must be flat, not sloping. You might choose:
- carpet
- tiled floor
- wooden floor
- concrete
- grass
- decking

2 Prop the wooden board against the pile of books to make a ramp on the first surface.

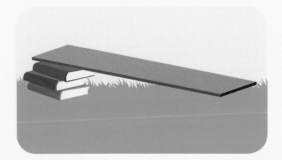

3 Put the rolling toy at the top of the ramp and let it go. Do not push it.

4 When the toy has stopped rolling, use the drinking straws to measure the distance between the bottom of the ramp and the toy's back wheels.

5 Record your measurement in a table like this:

Surface tested	Distance traveled in straw lengths	
	two and a bit	
grass		

6 Repeat steps 2 to 5 for the other surfaces.

What happens?

The rolling toy travels different distances on different surfaces.

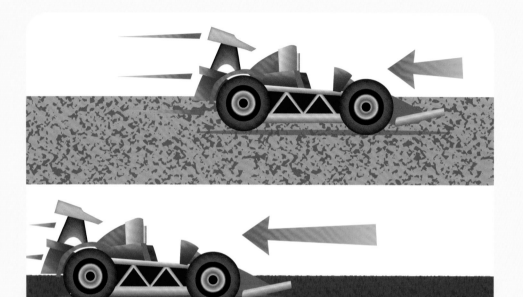

What do you think?

- On which surface does the rolling toy travel the farthest?
- Does this surface create the most friction or the least friction?
- Which surfaces create the least friction: rough surfaces or smooth surfaces?

How Forces Make Rolling Toys Work

This table shows some of the pushing and pulling forces that act on rolling toys.

Forces make toys . . .	Pushing or pulling force?	Example of the force acting on a toy
start moving	pushing force	An inline skate starts moving when a pushing force acts on it.
change direction	both	A bicycle changes direction when a turning force acts on its front wheel.
speed up	pulling force	A wagon speeds up when a pulling force acts on it.
slow down	pushing force	A skateboard slows down when the pushing force of friction acts on its wheels.
stop moving	pushing force	A toy car stops when a large enough impact force acts on it.

Glossary

axles   rods that pass through the middle of wheels, and work by holding the wheels in place and allowing them to turn

friction   a force that slows down moving objects, and acts in the opposite direction to the direction the object is moving in

gravity   the force that pulls objects toward Earth, and acts on everything, all the time

impact force   a force that acts on a moving object when it hits something

rolling   moving along the ground by turning one part (for example, the wheels) over and over

surfaces   the outside or top layers of things

turning force   a force that causes something to turn, made up of a pushing and a pulling force working together

wheels   round discs with an axle through the middle, which work by turning around the axle

Index